Life-Threatening

From the Diary
of a Victim of Bullying

SHERRY ROGERS

ISBN 979-8-88616-921-8 (paperback)
ISBN 979-8-88616-922-5 (digital)

Christian Faith Publishing
832 Park Avenue
Meadville, PA 16335
www.christianfaithpublishing.com

Printed in the United States of America

ACKNOWLEDGMENTS

This book is dedicated to my beloved son, Rodrecous Rogers, and to all of the children and adults who have been victims of bullying and to those who have lost their lives because of it. You are stronger than you think and more courageous than you know. Take your power back.

CONTENTS

INTRODUCTION

What do you think about when you hear the word *bully*? Do you think of someone who constantly physically or verbally threatens or intimidates others? Some people do not understand the damage they can produce with their words. In this book, I will show the significance and the importance of seeing bullying for what it is. It is life-threatening. The degree of pain bullies inflict on their victims can be unbearable. I was a victim of bullying. As a matter of fact, I had more in my life than I could stand. I can only speak my truth about how I went from seeing life as beautiful to seeing only the ugliness that being bullied brought to my life. Nice is hard to maintain when you are in the grips of a bully.

The meaning of bullying is to seek to harm, intimidate, or coerce someone perceived as vulnerable. What does *coerce* mean? It is to persuade an unwilling person to do something by using force or threats. *Life-threatening* means seriously dangerous and likely to result in death. Victims of bullying feel pressured and forced into making drastic decisions.

If we all look at the damage it causes, we will begin to see the need for stricter punishment wherever bullying takes place. Bullying has led to many suicides, and it has also driven its victims to carry out mass shootings of innocent children. While this act of violence is extreme, have you ever thought that the one being bullied is innocent? They never ask to be teased; all they want is to feel safe.

It is critical for all of us to take a closer look into the victim's mind to see how bullying leads to death. In this book, I will take you on a journey through a victim's mind so that you will know the signs of the bully, the victims of bullying, and the life-threatening effects of bullying. I will tell you where you should look and who we should be looking at.

Are you ready to take a ride with me? It will not be long, but it will be impactful.

CHAPTER 1

Life-Threatening

Life began to change for me when I was in the third grade. To me, life was beautiful. I was learning about new things like how the wind feels blowing on my face to the green grass, about the animals, and about different smells. All my senses were at work, and I loved everything I was experiencing. I would say I was happy and full of life. I did not have to be concerned about many things.

The walk from school to home was educational. I loved to observe, seeing life like I had not seen it before. Life for a child is supposed to be fun and educational. A young child is in an experiential phase of learning about life, ourselves, and others. We tend to be a bit naive, innocent, pure, and curious about many things during childhood. Parents are our first teachers. They are supposed to teach their children about life, its purpose, and how we grow and overcome adversity. As a child, I did not know what to expect; I just knew I loved life, but I was never told what to do when life became hard to bear. To my surprise, I would soon find out.

Miserable people seek to harm others, and bullies fit in this category of people. How long have bullies been around? I'm sure bullying existed before I was born, yet I never heard about it in school or anywhere else. I was in for a life-altering awakening. Someone may say victims of bullying are overexaggerating, weak, and cannot take the pain. Well, you are underestimating the cry for help. Stop and look inside the victim's mind and heart; listen with everything in you to hear their story. It may be hard to hear and understand the victim's perspective if you have not been through it.

School leaders have failed to stop bullying once and for all. I believe there is a solution, not just for school leaders but also for all who will listen and implement the proposed strategies against bullies. School leaders and others believe that if a bully is not physically harming you, you should be able to make up and move on. That is a mistake; most bullies continue to bully others.

The funny thing is that when victims become weary of the attacks, some think of ways to handle their bullies. When victims of bullying are pushed and coerced into taking matters into their own hands, the school looks to punish them instead of first punishing the bully. Bullies are armed and ready to shoot and cut up their victims with their tongues. The tongue is a weapon we can use to speak life or death to someone, cursing or blessings. How many have we killed with our tongue? Bullies use their tongues as weapons of mass destruction.

Can you look and listen to what I am saying? I have gone through it as a victim of bullying to give you more insight into this issue that has yet to be solved. Who is to blame for all the suicides, mass shootings, and other acts of violence? Who caused so much damage in our schools and destroyed us?

I want to share some of my experiences with bullies and how I overcame them. I pray this will give someone hope and tools on how to combat those who bully you. We must be aggressive and five steps ahead of the issue. We have taken the matter of bullying too lightly. It's past time to demand action and to take control of this issue.

Open your mind and eyes to see who killed or is killing your children. I demand we bring more safety to our schools, homes, and communities. The nation has come a long way but still needs help. We desperately need a law against bullying and consequences that will bring correction to their offense. In some cases, a bully may need to be rehabilitated in a juvenile correctional facility to learn that harming others will no longer be tolerated. This is the beginning of saving lives. Victims of bullying are most likely to go to jail before the bully does because the manifestation of bullying is violence. The victim interprets bullying as violent and eventually acts out in response to the violence. The truth is that it is violent, and until we recognize it from the victim's vantage point, we will continue to lose children to suicide and other violent acts.

CHAPTER 2

Self-Sabotage

Before I knew what suicide was, I already had thoughts of how I could end my life to escape those who were bullying me. The conclusion to end my life was easy because I would no longer be a problem to others. It is one thing to be under attack by others versus attacking yourself. The worst thing you could do is turn on yourself, but it's easy to do when you are tormented by others daily. Those who bullied me stole from me. My education had been threatened; they stole my peace, my safety, my voice. I had no self-esteem; the essence of who I was, was jeopardized. How can someone have that much power over me with words? They sought to sabotage me and everything about me. They were determined to come after me.

My bullies drove me to the point of handling them on my own, but I failed to find a permanent solution. All I wanted them to do was shut up and leave me alone, but instead, I eventually downloaded their voices in my memory. I could not get them out of my mind; somehow, they penetrated my inner circle, and they became a part of my daily life. Dealing with them in person was hard enough, but dealing with them in my head was a much-more-brutal fight. I allowed their words and accusations to override my own. They started dictating my life from within. I listened to what my bullies said about me, and I began to believe what they were saying.

I turned against myself in search of ways to disappear. I just wanted to die. It seemed to be the best option. I hated everything about me, my hair and feet, and I became upset with God, asking Him why he would make me like this. "Why would you make me ugly, bald-headed, talk funny, tall, have big lips, a big nose, and no nice clothes?" I know I complained to God every day asking why.

What I started doing was sabotaging my own life. I made decisions based on what my bullies said, coming into an agreement with their words. I continued to complain to God about everything, questioning his reason for bringing me into the earth. What is my purpose in life, and what do I do?

I realized in my adult life that I did all the talking to God about my life, and I came to the conclusion that God had been talking to me all the time. I did not recognize His voice until I slowed down in life. I was too busy complaining, and I never listened to God as he tried to get His messages to me. God gave me answers in some cases, and in others, I got them later when I became still.

Self-hate is far more deadly than any bully can be and this is one of the life-threatening consequences of bullying. I know now that I am somebody and that I have someone who loves me, will take care of me, nurture me, give wisdom, life, and peace to my soul, and He told me that I am his own. If you are under the attacks of others, pray to God to help you and he will. God will tell you all about you and that He created you in His image. He loves you, He cares for you, and He will put to flight those who oppose you.

God is a redeemer, and He will pluck you out of the enemy's snare. God will teach you how to fight and stand up for yourself in His power. We need His strength to stand. God will restore you when those who bully you take from you.

CHAPTER 3

Know Your Enemy

We must know who our enemy is in order to fight strategically. The enemy our soul has set out to kill us or take us into captivity. He will use anyone who will yield to his influence, even children. You may ask why it is important to know the enemy. The military is one way to look at it; soldiers are trained to know their enemy, where he is located, and his tactics. An enemy is a person or group that is actively opposed or hostile to someone or something. An enemy seeks to harm or weaken something or someone else. The enemy is intelligent, so do not underestimate their tactics. We must understand why the enemy is pursuing us with such violence.

Bullies are violent. They seek to harm and hunt down their prey to inflict pain, but they often seek to kill and do not realize it. I did not know my enemies and never understood why they came for me constantly. I did not know how to fight with words. I was uneducated about bullies and why they do the things they do. I know it starts somewhere why bullies are determined to attack others. Maybe just maybe they were bullied at home by parents or someone else outside of school. I know it has to start somewhere. Who taught them to be so mean and to say hurtful things?

I was completely unaware of the bullies' level of cruelty, and it took years before I learned how to deal with the trauma, and I am still fighting. A physical fight is easy to interpret and deal with, but it is another problem when the battle becomes spiritual. Spiritual fighting is hard and takes skill to do because the mind is under attack. Why do you think bullying can lead to suicide and even mass shootings? The victim is thinking about what they are going through and how to deal with it. We internalize everything and try to understand why; some of us deal with it daily and think about it daily. How do I get through this? It hurts so bad, and I do not want to feel this pain. My mind was occupied by the words and torment I faced daily. I had no room for anything else.

If I told you who the real enemy is, you would not believe it, but some will. The enemy is Satan; he is the bully of all bullies. As I stated earlier, he is the enemy of our soul and he will use anyone who is willing, knowing or unknowingly, to submit to his influence. He is the root we should be looking at.

His plans are strategic, and he knows how to work his plan. He executes his plan as soon as we are born, and he plans to destroy us before we get to our destiny. The Word of God says the thief came to steal, kill, and destroy. Who? Us! This is the result of bullying; it steals, kills, and destroys. The devil can use one person to take out a mass of victims. Bullying is an act of Satan, and we must look at this from a spiritual perspective as well.

I know it is true because I've experienced it for myself, and God revealed to me that it has been Satan all along and not just others who harmed me. When the trauma of bullying takes root, the damage continues even after the bullies are gone, and an all-out war starts inside of you. This is indeed life-threatening.

CHAPTER 4

The Cage

The cage was a place I went to in times of crisis. I created the cage to have a safe place to hide. The cage had bars like a prison cell, and its structure was square. It wasn't huge, but it had just enough space for a child to go in and out. The best part about it was that I had a key to open or lock it. I loved retreating to my place of refuge to keep myself from doing the unthinkable in retaliation against my bullies. I knew no one would be able to reach me, and I didn't want to be reached by anyone who wanted to hurt me.

The cage was warm and inviting, and I was the only one that had the key to it until I realized I wasn't. I had to lock myself away to keep the monster inside me from coming out and unleashing its wrath. I had become someone I did not want to be. I felt that I was driven to the point of insanity from the daily reminder that the bullies were coming. I had a choice to allow my dark side to come out or lock myself up to keep from hurting someone. Most of the time, I would not let the evil out, but the more I held back, the stronger my evil side became.

As I look at myself inside of the cage, I see I am broken, bloody, and crying out for help, but no one can hear me. I had some sense to hold back from doing the unthinkable, but it was hard to resist the urge over and over. I knew I was a kind person. I did not seek to harm others because I was not raised that way. The monster had become powerful, even more powerful than the good side of me; it would scream and argue with me, and it wanted total control of my mind.

The monster was full of anger and rage from being taunted by bullies over the years, and it wanted revenge; a small part of me did too, but I said no. I am a good person, and I do not want to be evil. My dark side would speak to me and tell me things to do to get even with all the bullies who tortured me. A lot of the thoughts I would disagree with because I refused to become a bully. I angered myself because I restrained my wrath, creating an all-out war between good and evil within me. I just wanted to die to end all the thoughts racing through my mind. If you have ever been bullied, then you understand how I felt.

The cage was necessary to keep the vengeful monster in and maintain the good part of myself that I wanted to protect from bullies. I thought I created a safe place for myself, but eventually, it became a prison for me and the monster. That's when I realized that I wasn't the only one with a key to the cage.

Satan had one too! He took what I created to protect others from my wrath and used it against me to restrict, ensnare, and lock me away permanently. I know parents who feel as if they have lost their children and think they are unreachable. They are right to think this way because the child has indeed become unreachable. Yes, they have made themselves inaccessible to you and whatever else is actually bothering them.

The creation of the cage was life-threatening because it was impossible to be inside the cage and live life fully present and conscious of the world around me. Children who create cages to hide away are in a crisis and are in need of emergency help. It is vital that we start to pray and listen to God for instructions concerning our children. Why do we as people think we do not need God to help us? God is our creator and He created humanity. We must look to Him to know how to dismantle all forms of bondage, even those that we created with the best intent in mind. The cage became life-threatening because now I had become imprisoned by Satan and needed God to deliver me.

CHAPTER 5

The Song

Music. Who do you know who does not like music? We all would love it if someone wrote a song about us. Of course, we would want the song to be positive, inspiring, and genuine.

The girls who bullied me daily did just that; they wrote a song about me. They decided to sing the song to me as we walked home from school. I knew they were up to something, but I did not know what it was. I thought they were going to jump me, and I was afraid and trembling in my shoes. I was looking for a way to escape. Should I run or be still?

The girls who taunted me in elementary school were also my bullies in middle school. Unfortunately, the walk home from middle school was much longer than the walk home from elementary school. The girls were relentless and persistent in talking about my hair. I tried to walk quickly to keep them at a distance. Sometimes I darted out the door at the sound of the bell to make my great escape. They were only a short distance away, and I did my best to keep them from catching up to me.

In the distance, I heard them singing a song about my hair repeatedly. I thought, *How dare they talk about me like that!* I was embarrassed, and I felt like dying because I could not take that song any longer. I do not know which one came up with that song, but their intentions were to humiliate me. These are the lyrics to the song: "A is for apple, J is for Jack, Sherry ain't got no hair in the back." I know it went on for at least a mile and a half. By this time, I was angry and frustrated; my peace was no more. I yelled at them to leave me alone over and over. When we got close to the top of Medaris Road, I turned around and started fighting.

I did not care anymore. Two sisters from the group of kids singing the song came for me, and we began throwing hands, which is to fight. I was determined to fight for myself, my peace, and my life. I did not want to go there, but they pushed me to the limit. That was the day I became the Incredible Hulk. I turned into a green rageful monster out to destroy anything that got in my way. That day, my bullies found out that they would not like me when I was angry.

That song, to me, and the writers were vicious in their attempt to destroy me. Right up to this present day, I have not been able to delete that song from my memory. So if you ask me, no, I do not want anyone to write a song about me, unless they wanted to build me up and not tear me down. I thought this fight was the end. I won, and I believed it was over, but not so fast. Something else was brewing in the air that same day.

CHAPTER 6

The Sticks

That same day, the two sisters went home and told their siblings about the fight. I went home, and I felt good about winning, but I do not remember telling my brother about the fight. I was glad it was over. I felt justified in my choice to fight. My family and I were at home that evening. My brothers, sisters, and I were playing and running around inside the house, and out of nowhere, I heard people outside yelling. My brother and I proceeded to look out the window and noticed a crowd of people in our yard. At this point, I was explaining to my brother why they were out there.

My brother did not want me to go outside, but I told him to let me go out to explain to the adults who had gotten involved why I fought them. Of course, my brother did not want me to go out, so he and I tussled back and forth. I was determined to go outside where they were standing. We noticed the crowd of people had sticks, and I thought I even saw bats. I was not afraid of them; I was at home, and I had more confidence and more power when I was home. I do not know why I would feel this way once I arrived home.

My brother wanted to protect us from whatever they came to do. They were so mad at me, but they never asked me what happened and why. They just wanted me to come outside. Why it took a whole family to come after me, I still don't know to this day. I could only imagine why. I was one person being jumped by two sisters, and that is not a fair fight. They had already bullied me for years, and I never tried to get them in any trouble. The sticks they carried had way less intimidation than the bullying itself.

While my brother was telling them to leave, they refused to do so. They wanted me badly. I wanted to go out and tell them what happened, but I didn't want to fight them. I wanted them to know that I had no choice and that I asked the girls to leave me alone over and over. They didn't care about me or my feelings; I thought if I could tell the crowd my story, they would leave our yard and go home, but they did not. They had made a big scene outside until one of our neighbors came out, put them out of our yard, and told them to go home.

I was not afraid of the crowd. The next day at school, I noticed some people from the crowd were watching me as I came on campus. I thought they were going to retaliate then, but they did not. I was suspended from school because of the fight; one of the girls went to the office that morning and cried about the fight. I know that she didn't mention the song, the bullying, or them chasing me home every day, and most likely she told lies about me, something she had done many times before. She was a bully in my life all the way to adulthood.

I was the only one suspended, and the principal never asked me what happened. That is why victims of bullying are punished most of the time while bullies go unchecked. This is indeed life-threatening.

CHAPTER 7

The Hat

One day, my mother decided to apply an S-curl to my hair. I was so excited about getting my hair done. I had a big smile on my face. I knew this was the moment when my hair problem would end. At one point in time, I thought my hair looked fine. Of course, it was short and nappy at times, but it was my hair, and I was okay with it.

After a while, I became very insecure because I was being teased about my hair; they would always call me Bald Head. I felt the need to keep my hair looking as good as possible, but the name-calling was still there. After my mother was done with my hair, she realized that it did not come out as expected. I was incredibly sad because I had no curls in my hair, and it was a disaster. I knew this was not good and that I had to find a way to hide my hair. I came up with the best solution I could think of before I went back to school. I chose to wear a hat to school, but

I never considered what would happen if one of the bullies tried to snatch it off or what if someone asks me to remove the hat. I was in for a rude awakening.

As class started, I sat in my seat, and the classroom was full of students. As the teacher started class, she began talking about our assignments. She started to look in my direction. I froze in my seat, and I could not breathe; I did not know what was about to happen. She noticed I had on a hat, and she asked me to remove it. Little did she know that I was hiding something underneath the hat.

The teacher began to ask me to remove my hat, and I shook my head no. We went back and forth about the hat, and I refused to remove it. Eventually, I gave in and began to remove my hat from my head gently and very slowly. All I thought about was what was under the hat, and I wore it thinking I'd be protecting myself from the mouth of others.

As all eyes in the classroom were on me, I felt as if a light was shone upon me. When the hat came off, the laughing started; all I could do was try to curl up inside myself. The sound of laughter was loud and intense, and I could barely breathe. I thought I would faint. When the teacher started laughing, I could not bear it anymore; as the tears flowed down my face, I was devastated.

Immediately I ran from the classroom to the bathroom, looked into the mirror at myself, and cried even harder. I knew I was never going to be the same. You would think that teachers would protect all their students rather than participate in a student's humiliation. The teacher called my mom to the school to get me out of the bathroom, but I could not go back into the room and look them in the eye. I was fed up with school and being around others. My hat was my protection from the humiliation, or so I thought.

When you are bullied, you think of ways to protect yourself from them; it did not work for me most of the time. Somebody may ask why I did not go to the principal's office or inform the school leaders about those that were bullying me. My answer would be that it was just as bad to tell on them as it would have made them mad and hurt me even more. When she did my hair, my mom did not know that I was already being teased about my hair. I could not share that with her, believing she would reject me. My hat was my protection and defense, or so I thought.

CHAPTER 8

The Threat

The first time I retaliated against someone else was not good. I became so fed up with everything that I allowed the evil side of me to come out. The voices in my head influenced me by reminding me of all the pain that my bullies had inflicted on me. I needed to get even, and I planned to put an end to all the bullying.

I did not want to feel anything but the emotions I tried to restrain from everyone who bullied me came rushing in. I decided to threaten an innocent person. She never bullied me; we were friends, and I enjoyed being around her. I had no reason not to trust her.

One day, she and I were outside riding on an ATV. It was a lot of fun until we were in an accident. My foot was slipping off the ATV. I yelled, telling her to stop because my foot was slipping. She continued to drive fast as if I didn't say anything. My foot slipped off, and the ATV tire rolled over it and then it was dragged through the gravel. I was injured and in a lot of pain. My foot had been ripped open, and blood was everywhere. At the time, I could only think about the pain. I was rushed to the hospital and was traumatized by the incident. I stayed in the hospital for several days and had to get surgery. Everything that I was experiencing in the hospital seemed scary; I did not know exactly what was happening.

When I got out, I began thinking that she caused the accident on purpose. I was so angry and wanted to end all attacks. Somehow, I decided that she was no different than my bullies. I wrote a letter threatening her life because I wanted her and my bullies to fear me. In my twelve-year-old mind, I believed that my threat would make them stay far away. I wanted my fifty feet of space and more.

Yes, I can admit I was homicidal and suicidal all at the same time. Fear can make you vulnerable and unstable. I knew I was in a dangerous situation at this point. The voices in my head were all negative. When you experience pain at the hands of another, you feel the need to get even. I know now that I sabotaged my true friendship based on what I had experienced with my bullies. She was innocent, but I was not able to distinguish the difference at the time.

Threatening another life is crossing the line. No matter how bad I felt, no one deserved my wrath, not even the ones who were bullying me. I realized I wanted to continue to be a good person in the midst of the pain. I can say this was a difficult journey to endure.

Earlier, I stated how we should know who the real enemy is. In my case, Satan was and is behind bullying, and his goal was to kill, steal, and destroy me. Think about it; bullying has resulted in death, and it steals and destroys people's lives. Clearly, this is the work of Satan. I will say that Satan has killed victims of bullying and innocent bystanders. My anger concerning bullying now is directed at Satan rather than people. Spiritual warfare for my life had become vital for survival. I thought the bully would kill me until God said to me that it is Satan who desires to sift you as wheat.

CHAPTER 9

MIP

My siblings and I changed schools quite often, so after going from school to school and dealing with bullies in each place, we finally settled in a new school district on the opposite side of town. I needed a change of environment to refocus. I was happy to get away from the bullies, and I hoped things would work out better for me. My past experiences with bullies wired my mind with trauma, abuse, humiliation, and anger, which is the mindset that I entered high school with.

In eighth grade, the volleyball coach invited me to try out for the high school volleyball team. I was excited that the coach would look at me as valuable. I did not look at myself the way the coach did. When I tried out for the volleyball team, I was not able to be fully present mentally. My mind and body did not line up together. So only part of me would be there in practice. The coach eventually pulled me to the side and said, "Sherry, if you do not get better, you will not make the team." I felt as if the coach was challenging me, so I took on the challenge and made the team.

While preparing for a new adventure in school, the students were not new to me. I examined the school body looking for the bullies from previous schools. I observed everyone, and I breathed a sigh of relief when not a single bully from the other district attended my new school.

I suffered from blackouts and blind spots in my memory. When I started high school, none of the bullies from my past were there, but eventually, new bullies emerged. I do not remember much about high school, but I recall that the bullying did not stop. To my surprise, I met new bullies, and most of them were males and a few were females. I could walk into a room and hear laughing, whispering, and sounds of students saying, "Ew!"

I found ways to get away from some people by hiding in the bathroom to skip class. I had fought a few times and landed in in-house suspension. I really liked that place because I was closed off from the rest of the school. I got in trouble on purpose just to escape the people that were bullying me. I do remember beating a boy down with my coat on the bus because he was always teasing me and spitting small pieces of balled-up paper at me; one had landed inside my mouth, and I was angry. We used to call them spitballs.

I know the only good moment in high school was when I received a trophy for most improved player (MIP). I improved in the sport of volleyball, but I had yet to grow and improve in life. I know now, mentally, I had already dropped out of school in elementary, and it manifested fully in high school. I did the least in studying to get by. I had become consumed by trauma and had no room for anything else.

The trauma from bullying had taken its toll on me and I was spiraling out of control. With the help of God, intense therapy, and the support of family and friends, I have since learned to put my best foot forward and strive to be a most improved player in the game of life.

CHAPTER 10

Overcoming the Trauma

The trauma resulting from bullying can be difficult to overcome, but you can live through it. I am a witness that you will come out only when you continue to fight. I barely made it through, only to realize I had suffered many scars. I was unhealthy mentally, and many days and nights, I cried. I wanted to remain a victim; it was too hard for me to grasp that one day I would overcome and come over to the other side of this issue. From my vantage point, it looked impossible. I was damaged to the very core of my soul, and when you are in pain mentally and spiritually, the doctor or emergency doctors cannot help you. This kind of pain takes time to heal, and you will need God to heal and restore you.

At the time, I could not express what I felt, but I see God protecting me as I look back. I was clearly on life support and have been in God's care for twenty-eight years. God supported me, and he kept me alive. Overcoming simply means to succeed in dealing with a problem or difficulty. During the time I was bullied, I did not understand any of it. It was foreign to me. As a young child, you want to know why, and that answer can be far from your mind. The pain was so loud inside of me that I could not focus on anything else. I would not be able to overcome that for which I was not equipped.

We must first understand why something is happening in order to overcome it because we cannot overcome what we do not understand. I could not overcome my trauma alone, but God had a plan for me, and He has a plan for you too. God is always concerned about us. Giving myself entirely to Jesus Christ was the start of a healing process and overcoming for me. Jesus said that He has already overcome the world and He has fought for us. Through the power of the Holy Spirit, He taught me how to fight. Through prayer and listening to the voice of God, I began to understand why I was being bullied, who was behind it, and my healing from the trauma would soon follow. The journey was not easy, but it was worth it.

You have to choose to overcome obstacles and challenges in life. People say what doesn't kill you can make you strong or weak, depending on your perspective on the issue. Why was all this trouble in my life, and why was it happening? Life is hard at times, but if you only stay in the race and endure until the end, you will overcome, and you will see that you have the power within you to make it. Satan is everyone's enemy, and he is always looking to devour us. His agenda is to keep us blind and ignorant and to keep us from overcoming. Jesus overcame and defeated Satan, and it is vital to look to Him for help so we can survive and overcome as well. I don't know about you, but I want everything God has for me to run my race.

CHAPTER 11

The Book

While I was writing and preparing this book, it has been revealed to me by God that even this book was locked away in a cage. It was through the process of exploring and working through my own trauma that I found a greater purpose in my life. Everything God has placed in us is destined to come forth, but we must be willing to show up for the assignment and do the work. Without a vision from God, we will perish. God has a plan and purpose for all of us, and what the enemy set in motion for our destruction, God is able to turn it around for our good.

Satan is the enemy of our soul, and his objective is total destruction. He will fight to prevent us from seeing and understanding the vision God has for us; he will even use bullies as his destructive agents. This is why the Bible says in the sixth chapter of Ephesians (NKJV), "We do not wrestle against flesh and blood."

In my case, the devil used the tactic of bullying early in my life to keep me blinded by people, pain, and frustration and to cut me off from everything that was good. I had to take back what belonged to me, including my purpose, future, and sanity.

For a season of my life, fear paralyzed me, and I lived in its grips daily. There were times when I couldn't move forward or backward and I didn't know if I should run or stand still. Fear ruled my life, but when I surrendered and gave my life back to God, His perfect love for me cast out all my fears. His love for me gave me a sense of security that I never had. It disarmed the words of every bully in my life and empowered me with self-love and self-worth.

When it comes to bullying, my revelation is this: Satan's strategy is to steal, kill, and destroy us even before we know who we are. We must keep fighting no matter what, and when we feel overwhelmed, it is always best to tell somebody. If you are suicidal, seek help until they listen to you, and never give up on yourself. God says He knows the thoughts He thinks toward you, thoughts of peace and not of evil, to give you a future and a hope (Jeremiah 29:11). Remember this: "Life and Death lies in the power of the tongue" (Proverbs 18:21). Those who bully others speak of death and violence; this is so obvious as we all see the results of what bullying has caused in so many lives.

My heart has been broken so many times when I hear about children taking their own lives and the ones who retaliate and go on shooting sprees in our schools. I understand the emotional trauma all too well. Our future and our children are in grave danger. It is time to take a stand to prevent the destructive patterns of bullies and save lives. How do we do this? We start by listening to our children, having discussions in our home about bullying, and not minimizing the hostile words and acts of others. We must pay attention to the patterns of behavior that might indicate that someone is a bully or is a victim of bullying and take action immediately.

Let's commit to taking a stand against bullying and limit its threat to the lives of our children.

ABOUT THE AUTHOR

S herry Rogers was born and raised in the beautiful city of Huntsville, Alabama. She is the proud mother of five children (one daughter and four sons), and the grandmother of three baby girls.

As a managing licensed cosmetologist, Sherry makes people feel beautiful and loved. Her gentle and quiet spirit is her unfading beauty, of great worth before God.

Sherry is a minister of the gospel and a mighty intercessor. Her passion for Christ and sharing the message of the cross precedes everything that she does.

Life-Threatening is her first book, and there are more to come.